Take-Off!

Lives and Times

MOHANDAS GANDHI

John Barraclough

Heinemann
LIBRARY

www.heinemann.co.uk

Visit our website to find out more information about Heinemann Library books.

To order:

☎ Phone 44 (0) 1865 888066

🖹 Send a fax to 44 (0) 1865 314091

💻 Visit the Heinemann Bookshop at www.heinemann.co.uk to browse our catalogue and order online.

First published in Great Britain by Heinemann Library,
Halley Court, Jordan Hill, Oxford OX2 8EJ,
a division of Reed Educational and Professional Publishing Ltd.
Heinemann is a registered trademark of Reed Educational and Professional Publishing Ltd.

OXFORD MELBOURNE AUCKLAND
JOHANNESBURG BLANTYRE GABORONE
IBADAN PORTSMOUTH (NH) USA CHICAGO

Designed by Ken Vail Graphic Design, Cambridge
Illustrated by Shirley Tourett
Originated by Dot Gradations
Printed by South China Printing in Hong Kong/China

ISBN 0 431 13440 5 (hardback)   ISBN 0 431 13445 6 (paperback)
05 04 03 02 01   05 04 03 02 01
10 9 8 7 6 5 4 3 2 1   10 9 8 7 6 5 4 3 2 1

British Library Cataloguing in Publication Data

Barraclough, John
  Mohandas Gandhi. – (Lives and times) (Take-off!)
  1.Gandhi, M. K. (Mohandas Karamchand), 1869–1948 – Juvenile literature
  2.Statesmen – India – Biography – Juvenile literature
  3.Pacifists – India – Biography – Juvenile literature
  I.Title
  954'.035'092

Acknowledgements

The publishers would like to thank the following for permission to reproduce photographs: The New York Times, p. 22; Topham Picturepoint, pp.18, 19, 20, 21.

Cover photograph reproduced with permission of Hutton Getty.

Our thanks to Sue Graves and Hilda Reed for their advice and expertise in the preparation of this book.

Every effort has been made to contact copyright holders of any material reproduced in this book. Any omissions will be rectified in subsequent printings if notice is given to the publishers.

Contents

Any words appearing in the text in bold, **like this**, are explained in the Glossary.

Childhood

Mohandas Gandhi was born in India in 1869, over 130 years ago. When he was a little boy, he was afraid of the dark.

night-light

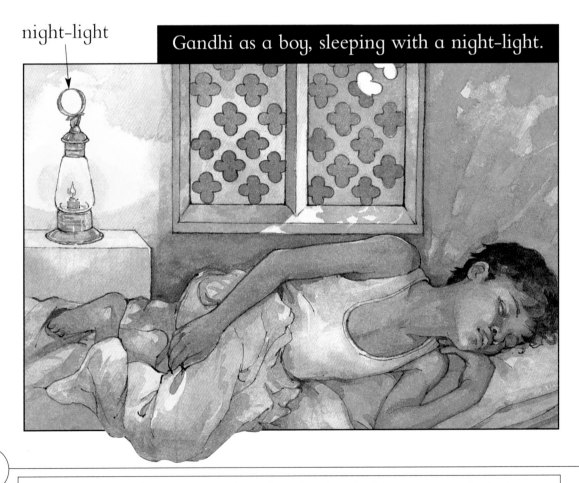

Gandhi as a boy, sleeping with a night-light.

Gandhi was born in Porbandar in the Indian state of Gujarat.

Gandhi

Kasturbai

Gandhi and Kasturbai's wedding.

Gandhi's family were **Hindus**. When he was thirteen he had an **arranged marriage**. He did not choose his wife. He and his wife Kasturbai did not live together until they were adults.

Work

In 1888, when he was nineteen, Gandhi went to London to learn how to be a **lawyer**. He was often lonely and homesick for India. He missed his wife Kasturbai.

Gandhi

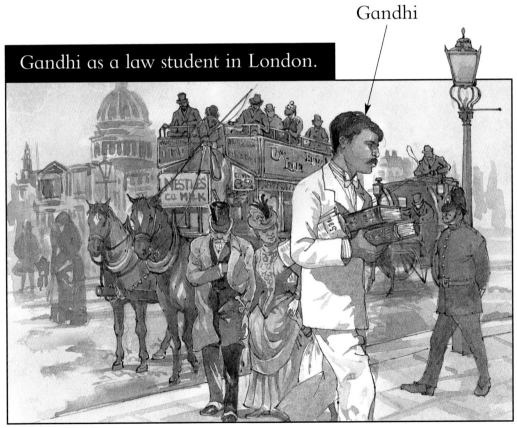

Gandhi as a law student in London.

Gandhi being thrown off the
train because he was Indian.

In 1893 Gandhi went to work in South Africa.
One day, he was thrown off a train because
another passenger hated Indians.

Fighting racism

This **racism** made Gandhi angry. He began to fight racism, but peacefully. One day, he stopped police horses charging at a crowd by making everyone lie on the ground.

Gandhi knew that the horses would not want to step on people.

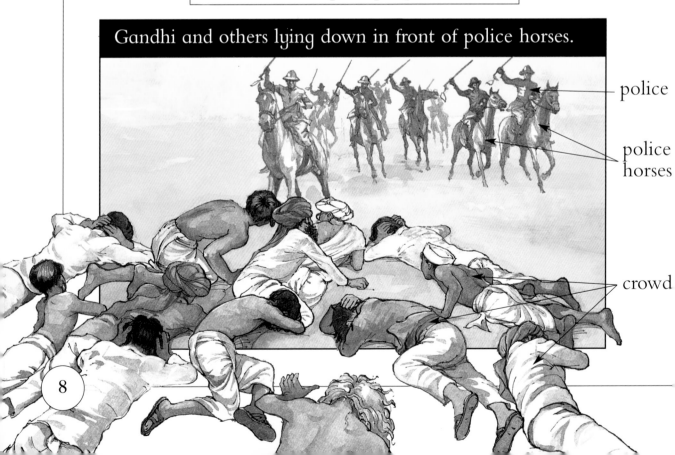

Gandhi and others lying down in front of police horses.

police

police horses

crowd

crowd

Gandhi

Gandhi being greeted like a hero on his return to Bombay.

In 1915 Gandhi went home to India. Many people had heard of his good work. When his boat landed at Bombay he was treated like a hero.

Gandhi was given the nickname Mahatma, which means 'Great Soul'.

Britain ruled India

Britain **ruled** over India at the time. Many Indians did not like this. In 1919 British soldiers shot a crowd of 400 peaceful **protesters**. Gandhi believed that British rule had to end.

The soldiers shooting the crowd of peaceful protesters.

protesters

soldiers

Gandhi led a Salt March because there was a tax on salt and nobody was allowed to produce their own!

Gandhi leading a peaceful meeting.

Gandhi became a great leader for the Indian people. He organized many peaceful meetings to show the British that they should leave India and stop ruling there.

Trying to change things

In 1931 Gandhi went to Britain to talk to the Prime Minister. He agreed with many of Gandhi's ideas, but still said that the British would not leave India.

Gandhi at 10 Downing Street in London to talk to the Prime Minister.

The Prime Minister in 1931 was a man called Ramsey Macdonald.

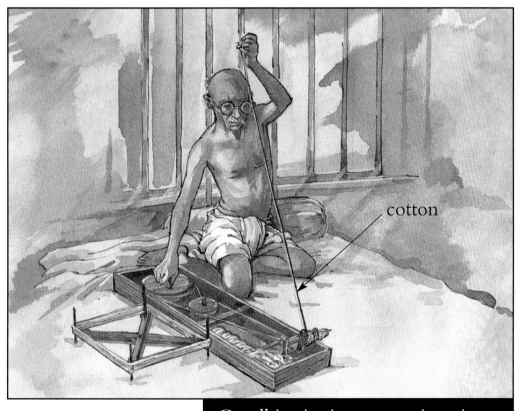

cotton

Gandhi spinning cotton in prison.

When he got home to India, Gandhi was
arrested for trying to change things. During
his life he spent a total of seven years in
prison. He passed the time thinking and
spinning cotton.

Independence

On 15 August 1947, the British left India. India became **independent**. The Indians could fly their own flag at last. This huge country was then split into two countries, India and Pakistan.

The flag which was flown when India became independent.

India became a **Hindu** state and Pakistan became a **Muslim** one

Gandhi

gunman

Gandhi on his way to pray.

Many people all over the world loved Gandhi and had agreed with his ideas to make India independent. Yet on 30 January 1948, a gunman killed him as he went to pray.

Funeral

Gandhi's last words were 'Hay Rama'. This means 'Oh God'. The Indian prime minister said: 'The light has gone out of our lives and there is darkness everywhere.'

flowers

Gandhi   mourners

Gandhi was India's greatest leader. His ideas are still admired and needed today.

All of his life, Gandhi never showed anger or hatred.

Mourners at Gandhi's funeral.

Photographs

This photograph shows Gandhi when he was seven. He was a shy boy. His mother was very religious and taught him to always be truthful and think of others.

Gandhi as a boy.

Gandhi

Gandhi with his friends at the vegetarian club in London.

Gandhi was **vegetarian**. This photograph shows him in London in 1890 with members of a vegetarian club where he made friends.

In London and South Africa, Gandhi wore a smart suit. When he was 44 he decided to dress simply, like most Indians at the time.

Gandhi dressed in simple cotton clothes.

simple cotton clothes

factory
workers

Gandhi

Gandhi with British factory workers.

Gandhi was very popular with ordinary people. This photo shows him laughing and joking with factory workers in Britain in 1931.

Reports and artefacts

This news report from an American newspaper is about Gandhi's **fasting**. It shows that he was ready to starve himself to death to get laws changed.

The report in *The New York Times* about Gandhi's fasting.

news report

The New York Times.

Copyright, 1932, by The New York Times Company.

d as Second-Class Matter,
office, New York, N. Y.

NEW YORK, WEDNESDAY, SEPTEMBER 21, 1932 ★★★★ + TW

M'KEE SAYS BANKERS FORCE BUDGET CUTS; DR. NORRIS RESIGNS

Loans to Stop if $80,000,000 Is Not Slashed, Aid Pledged for Public Works if It Is.

MAYOR ACCEPTS ULTIMATUM

"Determined" to Get Economy, He Repeats—Office Working Nights to Rush Schedules.

NORRIS QUITS IN PROTEST

Medical Examiner Resents 20% Cut for Bureau—City Gets Offer for Model Housing Development.

Forging ahead yesterday toward budget economy as a means of obtaining further loans from the bank-

CURRY AND M'COOEY

Gandhi, Tired and Ill, Begins His Death Fast After Hearty Meal and Prayer for Strength

Wireless to THE NEW YORK TIMES.

BOMBAY, Sept. 20. — Mahatma Gandhi solemnly began his "fast unto death" today behind the walls of Yerovda jail at Poona.

Exhausted by the strain of the past few days, the 63-year-old Mahatma was ill and under a doctor's care as he started his fateful hunger strike. He has had heavy correspondence and a colossal number of telegrams to deal with ever since he announced he would starve to death as a protest against the government's communal settlement. In view of his condition, the prison physician decided not to allow visitors to see him this morning.

All over India Hindus ceased work. Thousands went to the temples to pray for the Mahatma. Other thousands shuttered their shops or stayed away from their work at the factories as a gesture of sorrow.

Mr. Gandhi had a substantial meal before beginning his long, slow ordeal. He had his usual dates, soaked in water, and with them he ate whole-meal bread, tomatoes, oranges and curd. Then, visibly agitated, his secretary, Mahadev Desai, handed him a glass of lemon juice and soda.

This was the last sustenance he will touch, except for water.

When his last meal was finished, the Mahatma quietly announced his fast had started, and knelt to pray, with Vallabhai Patel, the All-India Nationalist Congress leader, and Mr. Desai kneeling alongside him.

A strangely subdued tension gripped the big Hindu centres of India as his fast began. Bombay's Hindu business quarters were deserted. The cotton and bullion markets and the Stock Exchange were closed. Nineteen cotton mills had to suspend because their workers failed to appear. Many schools and colleges were forced to shut their doors because so few students reported for classes. In the European and Moslem quarters, however, business went on as usual without interference.

The most significant event of the day was the admission of the "untouchables" for the first time to certain Hindu temples in Bombay, Nasik and Ahmedabad.

Despite the opposition of the ortho-

Continued on Page Eight.

FINDS RACKETS COST

LA FOLLETTE BEATEN IN WISCONSIN FIGHT; DR. LOVE LOSES HERE

Kohler, Conservative, Named for Governor—Youngman Leads in Bay State.

MRS. PRATT WINS IN CITY

McCooey Man Defeats Dr. Love in State Senate Race—Hastings Renominated.

MIX-UP OVER BALLOTS HERE

Patrolman and Boy Are Shot in Dispute at Polls—Roosevelt Scores Victory Up-State.

Voters in New York, Massachusetts and Wisconsin went to the polls yesterday for the last of the State

22

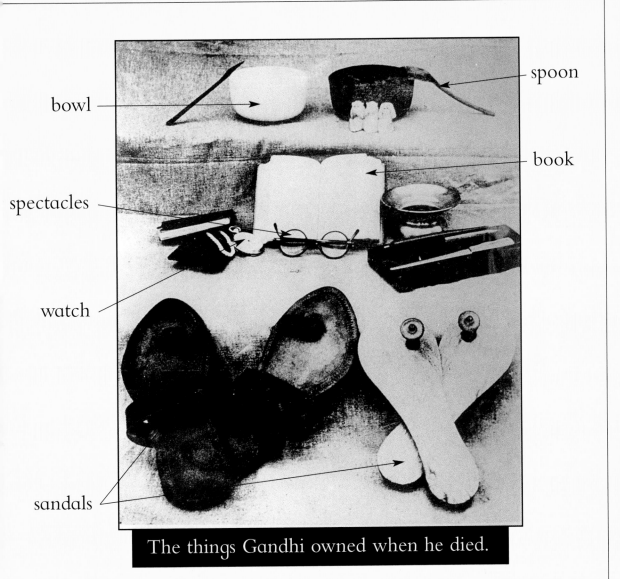

bowl

spoon

book

spectacles

watch

sandals

The things Gandhi owned when he died.

Gandhi believed in living simply. This picture shows the few things he owned when he died. They were only worth about £2.50.

Glossary

arranged marriage when a person marries someone who is chosen by their parents

artefacts things which people make and use, like tools, clothes and cooking pots. We can learn about the past by looking at old artefacts. You say *arty-facts*.

fasting not eating anything

Hindu follower of Hinduism, one of the main world religions. Hindus believe that if you lead a good life, you will be re-born as a better person. You say *hin-doo*.

independent free

lawyer person who has studied the rules of a country

mourners people who are very sad about somebody's death

Muslim follower of Islam, one of the main world religions. You say *muz-lim*.

protester someone who shows publicly that they disagree with something, usually a rule

racism hating somebody just because they are from a different country or have a different colour of skin

rule be in control

vegetarian someone who does not eat meat or fish

Index